COLORS

COLORS

Visions Continually Flowing Within My Mind's Eye

June Clyder Carney

iUniverse

COLORS
Visions Continually Flowing Within My Mind's Eye

iUniverse books may be ordered through booksellers or by contacting:

iUniverse
1663 Liberty Drive
Bloomington, IN 47403
www.iuniverse.com
1-800-Authors (1-800-288-4677)

ISBN: 978-1-4917-2587-0 (sc)
ISBN: 978-1-4917-2588-7 (e)

Library of Congress Control Number: 2014904482

Printed in the United States of America.

iUniverse rev. date: 01/06/2015

Dedication

This book is dedicated to my sisters, Audrey and Gail who have always had my back. I love you very much.

Acknowledgments

There are so many people who not only supported me throughout the years leading up to this exciting moment, but truly inspired my creative spark to continue producing my writing. Therefore, I'd like to take this opportunity to thank them.

If you believe in miracles, as do I, then you will definitely understand my gratitude. I sincerely thank my Heavenly Father, for without Him I would not exist!

To my Beloved Parents and my Beloved Brother . . . the "Dreamer", "Strategist" and my "Baseball Partner", I hope I've made you proud and know how much that I love and miss your presence. And to my precious Son, Ronald J. Carney, Jr., whose intellectual accomplishments and philosophy on how The Family Unit blends is so awesome that it provokes me to envy! My love constantly flows for your continued love and support for me throughout this entire process. You are so special!!!

I would like to acknowledge my Sisters, Audrey and Gail, for their never-ending reinforcement that my life was, indeed, worth that extra "push"! Thank you for supporting me as well as keeping me on the "straight and narrow". I realize that I didn't always make your jobs easy.

To George, for without your dreadful talks over the years, my life would have been totally isolated from myself as well as my Family's. I will never be able to thank you enough for your tough love techniques. I love you "Bro"!

Lan, if it wasn't for your time and patience, I never would have memorized the "Preamble" in order to pass 8th. Grade History! I still remember how you came and joined me on the dining room rug and we practiced endlessly until I finally got it. 1969 was a long time ago, but I never forgot how you took the time to help me. Thanks once again!

To my generous, kind, and loving Grandchildren. Thank you for taking care of and supporting me in ways I couldn't even imagine. I love being your Grandma!

To my Daughter-in-Law for your love, caring ways and endless support as well as long hours working with and for me! I will always be grateful for your kind heart.

I am deeply grateful to Nancy, Denise, Mary Ann, Anne, Maureen, Carol Tassone, "My Timbo", Marin and Dave, Elizabeth Wilson Fomby M.D., "Duffensmirtz" and "Smartellica" for their vision, commitment and continuing Unknown Desire to be Catalysts in providing the world with Enlightenment. Also to my Texas family at Raintree . . . Brenda, Dale, Laveern, Ray and Roberta.

Thanks to Lanny Shaw Jr., Architect, for the inspiring cover design. You gave the book the "Polish" it needed! I absolutely loved it at first sight. I owe you one!

To "my mentors" Kari Carpenter and Shelley Kaufman Ph.D. I hope you really know how much you've helped me. You both have suffered through years of me digging through every emotional skeleton in my closet over the past 23 years and it has been tough on all of us! Thanks for your understanding and allowing me space to succeed. I couldn't have ever imagined being blessed with anything as awesome as the two of you.

I want to thank my nieces and nephews and their families for their support and encouragement and for all of your very kind and uplifting words of praise while I was on a mission to find myself!

To all of you, my book is for the humble people with a conscience and kind hearts . . . For those who care about other people . . . Most of all for those of you who want to know and understand that it was God who held my hand steady when I was at my weakest and gently when my words flowed ever so smoothly.

With All the Love a Heart Can Hold

To say how much we love you
Would be an understatement
Let alone begin to express how much you will be missed by all,
Many of the circles formulated in our lives,
Were held together by your presence.
However;
While our circles are lacking substance at the moment,
You have taught us throughout the years
How to be "masters" of our own thoughts, and
Through that knowledge
We will do just fine in continuing onward
Where you left off!
Oh, we know
You would not want the tears to keep flowing
During our time of sorrows,
Rather laughter and joy
Of the memories you have left behind.
But, for today let us mourn in our grieving
And in return, our tomorrows will make you even more proud
That when you were here to help in the sharing,
For the love you have given
Will enable each and every one of us
To become better individuals.

Sitting alone
just me and my stare
knowing all along
that you're always there
deep down
throughout the thoughts
in my mind
I believe with enough time
my answer
I will find
And as I go on staring
out the window I will see
the beauty of your face
just a smiling down
at me
I love you
oh so deeply
and it's growing
day by day
so whenever you have
a moment's time
walk down the path
that goes my way
and please
don't keep a pace
behind—
for I long to see your face
other than in my mind!

Dedicated
To My Son
Ronald J. Carney, Jr.

To Watch You Grow . . .

For so long now, I've watched you grow,
and I sometimes wonder how you really are.
At times you shine
and once you even cried.
Still it let me love you even more . . .

And I wonder now as I'm looking back,
exactly why I became so frightened
of your beautiful face
and your glowing smile
and the love you project for all of life to share.

You must have known then that I'd have to reach out
and purposely discard the realms of protection
that encased my mind,
and blinded my soul
to the violation of life called convenient stagnation.

I suppose it just takes a while to understand this life
and to be totally enveloped, before you can give
an expression of your soul
without being frightened
of the love that returns and is yours alone . . .

Oh the days blossom fuller and never seem to slow
their shuttle-bus pace, as I try to catch up.
When even the silence
seems to get louder
I can feel my soul struggle in a burst of expression.

For so long now, I've watched you grow,
and I could cry with love as I let you know
how much you've done
to teach me life;
and that it doesn't really matter that I was once so frightened.

And it occurs to me to just love you even more . . .
My Awesome Son!

Dedicated
To
"My Family"
June 29, 2010

Did you ever see a small child
preoccupied with an inadement object
and say to yourself
"I'd give anything to know what she's thinking"

So it is with adults …
I have no questions
nor second thoughts
about my destination
it's my life
and my love will grow much deeper
in the years to come

I want you to smile and be happy for me
simply pretend that I'm on an extended vacation …
don't look back with hesitation.
because I will always be with you in heart

I will not say good bye
for this is not the end.
I am moving … like many others …
to a new home and familiar surroundings

just as the small child above
my "objective" is my family—
and even though miles will separate us
I will still relive our visits and small talks that we have always shared.

With Immeasurable Appreciation
I Dedicate This
To Kari G. Carpenter

For tirelessly answering the questions,
for pioneering and supporting,
for keeping me on track throughout the learning process,
for understanding,
and finally,
for maintaining humor & balance through it all.

There will always be a solidarity
for demonstrating no limit to your patience
or ideas,
contributions in displaying talents
and, for sticking with me . . .
mostly, for continuing your excellence in
all phases of the work force
with practicality and fun.

I have never known
any other "Mentor"
on improving personal
effectiveness,
to generate such an overwhelming
positive reaction . . .
with power, conviction and feeling!

The ethical basis for human relations
defined a way of life,
not just a "methodology"
for the chance to
have a successful career.

      The principles you've taught
      have made a difference
      in my life.

With the Pride one Holds Dearly
For That of a Best Friend,
I Thank You . . .

For The Professional Wisdom Shared
In An Industry Encompassed
With Never-ending Complexities

For the laughter and the tears,
the worries as well as fears,
you will never be forgotten.

For the struggles to survive,
and success
with "well wished" pride,
the time has finally come,
for me to step aside . . .

Memories that we have shared
are "steadfast" in my mind
and throughout the years ahead,
hold tight
to the words being said,
for it is inevitable
that our paths will cross once again . . .
as the day will surely come
when I walk back inside
the grounds I have become accustom to.

However,
today must begin a newness
as I take a deep breath
and sigh . . .
to avoid my heart from breaking,
since the sorrow felt through crying,
needs time to resolve itself
and subside.

Dedicated
with
Honor and Admiration
to
Barbara B. Gimbel

"I Love You "Duff"

I love you for what you are
and for what you have given me.
I love you for being strong
and for protecting me in times of need.
I love you for seeing the light
and for showing me the bright side of living.
I love you for merely existing
and for letting me exist too!
I love you.

and who do I thank
for enabling this wonderful
emotion
to expand
way beyond the normal limits?

All these questions
All pertaining to you
So many dreams
Constantly being planned
And
Seen come true.
All my life
I've waited
To find an equal
Who I could share with,
And
Care with,
And
Love with.
That day has come
Reality has shown its true colors
Because
The very first night
Our eyes connected
Opportunity knocked
And
I allowed the door to be opened within myself.

The Untitled Poet

You have touched my life so unexpectedly,
that I am at a loss for words . . .
> *It's as though*
> *a mirror of images gone by*
> *are reflective*
> *of the individuals*
> *we represent.*

As if within my soul
you have reached your hand
into the depth
of the inner most being,
vacillating
beforehand,
allowing for an unrestricted flow in your approach.
> *At times, we have "connected"*
> *unexpressed, yet instantaneously aware*
> *of what had transpired.*

Too many "similarities",
identical in nature,
while our professions run separately;
however,
parallel emotionally . . .
as we formulate the basis
enabling the foundation to settle
throughout the structuring of our respective characteristics.

Questions,
continually unanswered,
for the unknown
is the missing link in the chain,
which one another thrives upon.

. . . And,
unless interference is given accessibility,
the unification experienced
will remain
infinite.

Dedicated to
Shelley Kaufman, Ph.D.

An emotional person
isn't always stable, but
he grasps onto life with
a far greater appreciation. He
lives, feeling change in his
heart.

—to those of you who have touched me in such a miraculous way,
I thank you & I love you
For your support
of
My Life's Journey
Through the
Use of
Words.
It's also what
Each one did
For me on a
Personal
Level . . .
My "dreamer",
My sensitivities
My son
My childhood
My addictions
My passion
To write—

My creativity
is my own!!!

To My Loved Ones

After 4 years
I finally pulled through!
I've walked—run—stumbled
and even hit rock bottom
before being content with myself.
I made it and I'm proud
but not only with my success—
because I had a lot of help,
moral support,
and most of all
a second chance.
I had to prove the real me
the me I didn't even know existed
until just recently . . .
I don't remember ever praying so hard
for God to give me the strength
so I wouldn't fail a second time
and, He must have heard me
because I'm still here,
When I look back
I recall the odds of a clean victory
and wonder how I made it.
It's fresh in my mind
the day I realized what I had done
to you, myself, and all the others . . .
but even though
I try to smile with thanks and happiness.

"Liquor"

it's recognized
as a cop-out
and even though
you refer to it
with consistency . . .
when difficulty comes along!

after awhile
it becomes a challenge
whether you admit it or not

IF you get hurt
it's eased
IF you get aggravated
it's eased!

you're testing yourself . . .
consuming a little more
with each depression.

In Loving
Memory
-2001—

"PS I Never Promised You A Good Piece . . . Of Writing"

THE POET IN ME HAS FAILED
WHAT ELSE CAN I DO
THE WORDS ARE NOT
FLOWING
IN THE DIRECTION
OF YOU . . .

MY NIGHT IS SO EMPTY
WITHOUT YOUR SMILING FACE
THE HALLS ARE SO DESERTED
IT'S A PITY
A REAL DISGRACE . . .

THE HOURS
THEY'RE LIKE DAYS GONE BY
AND THE URGE TO EMBRACE
WILL SHORTLY DIE
AND IF YOU'RE NOT HERE
NEITHER WILL I
TO SHARE IN THE MOST BEAUTIFUL
FULFILLING HIGH . . .

THE PILLS
THEY AREN'T A POPPING
MY HEART BEAT
SIMPLY QUIT HOPPING
AND EVEN THE COFFEE
ISN'T THE SAME

SINCE I CAN'T ASSOCIATE
ANYTHING ELSE WITH YOUR NAME . . .
BECAUSE
YOU'RE NOT HERE
AND THERE'S NOBODY TO BLAME . . .

SO, I'LL JUST QUIETLY SIT
HOLDING IN THE TEARS
WISHING DEEP WITHIN
THAT YOU'LL SOON RETURN TO SHARE WITH ME A GRIN!!!

And With That
First Kiss

It's as though the 4TH of July came early this year.
Fireworks exploding in my head,
Beautiful star bursts being displayed in the sky,
And at that precise moment, I felt 18 years old all over again.
Even though my surroundings were familiar,
My emotional state of mind brought back immense feelings
Of yesteryear!
Happiness, contentment and the sense of a potential love affair
Struck my inner most being.
Since that place in time I have experienced such joy,
And a bewilderment all at the same time.
For I never expected to engage in a world of
Human intensification in this lifetime again!

Christmas From The Heart, Year Round

A freedom, strong sensitivity, and a sense of power
generated out of an emotion, yet extremely controlled.

A gift . . . a keepsake . . . to be treasured a lifetime
far greater than monetarily.

A part of oneself, coming from deep within.

I give to you
without hesitation—
no need for second thoughts or preplanned details.
I truly enjoy
"Spontaneity"
and you have a natural talent for bringing out such want.

"Extravagant" & "Abundant"
are effective adjectives,
yet,
so often their placement abuses the initial meaning
behind an action.

Interference where my choice of selection is involved
becomes intolerable,
and my drive becomes predominant
until my efforts reach a state of satisfaction
allowing another masterpiece
to be enjoyed by you . . .
And when that precise moment evolves
I become elated with happiness!

AlShel-der

A fine line running through "who" you are
And "what you represent.

The distinction,
sometimes appearing vague,
lacks insight . . .
allowing a definite "parallel" to merge into one . . .
creating a barrier for separation in determining
the allowances for such a split
to occur
without reservations.

Portraying, as well as preserving
two distinct entities
becomes overwhelming
once "personal emotion"
overrides
professionalism . . .
causing an altercation of viewpoint.

Bobbie Socks
And Ball Bearings

Maybe the "Entire Wing"
Was a bit too much to ask for
However, a "Hallway" would be thoughtful.
If only it could be viewed
from my perspective.
Replacing wheels on my "roller skates"
Becomes quite expensive
In-part because I purchase top of the line
merchandise.
In-vision the various places I need to be
In order to see my Patients in a timely manner.
It's "extremely bothersome"
As a Physician,
When my Patients have to wait for me.
There is no excuse for such an
"Occurrence to happen".
Is there?
To introduce certain clauses
Is the preface for requesting
My own "hallway"
Which would be beneficial for everyone involved.

The White Picket Fence Insirational

Boundaries with enclosures
Enabling security of one's inner being . . .
With such preciseness.
Captivating the etched markings in the wood,
Allowing beauty within its confines,
One attempts to avoid the "emotional roller coaster"
Of its presents.

Are there limitations to the beauty?
It is often questioned if the boundary inside
Is invisible to the naked eye.

During moments of extreme stress
The boundaries begin the process of shrinking,
To protect against the pain created once entrance occurs.
Therefore, in so doing
The Fence begins to swarm inward.

How desperately do you want that
White Picket Fence?
I think it best to shop around for a while,
Until the price is within my "Emotional Range"!

Look closer—

Your smile tells my face
You're happy with what you see—
Your hands tell mine
Take hold—
Your arms wrapped 'round me
Tells me I'm safe—
Your body lying next to mine breathes rhythmically
Telling mine you're content—
Your body talks to mine
If you listen carefully
You'll hear mine answer . . .

Lenity

The waves, continually splashing onto the shore, causing the outcry of the winds to diminish in the distance, far beyond the shadows of darkness were heard for miles from the sea! The beauty within, captivating the outlines of our bodies, as the full moon kindled tenderly down upon the nakedness of our stance. There was a sudden pause of life as we gazed into one another's eyes, and at that moment, it became evident that what had taken place outside the boundary of our hideaway was incapable of invading our minds long enough to deprive us of the love we once shared. With that knowledge, silence became thunderous!!! . . . and the aftermath was overwhelmed with utter bliss since the specialness of "the bond" delicately created was insurmountable. However, a sudden twinge existed for humanity, as the vast majority would never experience such an intensity out of ignorance with regard to the emotional capacity within one's self which eventually deteriorates since the "soul" wasn't fully allowed to grow in a current of freedom naturally given at birth. The euphoria being expressed enabled me to expand my internal belief; thereby, not only accepting love but giving it back in return. This sense of freedom attributed to the confidence in my declaration of the happiness I have obtained without default!!!

Mind Games

I WOULD IMAGINE THAT THE TEST IS ON RIGHT NOW—NEVER ENDING—AS I RE-READ YOUR LINES, I BECOME MORE ENGROSSED IN THE CHARACTER YOU'VE PORTRAYED. IT'S NOT EASY TO CATCH YOU DORMANT, LONG ENOUGH TO MAKE A FINAL DECISION AS TO WHAT I TRULY FEEL IS GOING ON IN YOUR MIND—

GRANTED, YOU'RE NOT A "BABY SOUL," BUT AT TIMES, YOUR POWER IS SO STRONG THAT I FEEL LIKE THE "BABY SOUL!" MAYBE SOMETHING PREVENTS ME FROM COMPLETELY PIN-POINTING YOU, AS WELL AS THE PERSON YOU STAND FOR. IS IT POSSIBLE THAT THE CARING FACTOR IS PLAYING AN EXTREMELY IMPORTANT ROLE IN THIS? I DON'T FEEL THREATENED, RATHER HONORED BY THE STYLE IN WHICH YOU CHOOSE TO COMMUNICATE—

BUT STILL, I HESITATE AND ASK MYSELF SOME QUESTIONS FROM TIME TO TIME. I REALIZE THAT THIS ACTION ISN'T ABNORMAL, BUT, THE QUESTIONS HAVE ALREADY BEEN ANSWERED SEVERAL TIMES OVER.

An Outcry for Understanding

People are seldom straight—
they're full of hang-ups
and past experiences.
It can be hell
to break the barrier
of years environmental phases.
You have little to work on
and scarcity where co-operation comes in.
Sometimes it's like fighting a war,
that took place centuries ago—
Death before Birth!
It can be quite difficult
to even speak those first words—
but if you don't begin
there can't be a victory of the smallest sort.
The choice is yours
and if by chance
it doesn't work out
It's your loss . . .

"With luck"

so it's been said that we can't have everything,
for as I tried
i failed
but not without the pride of winning.
you say it's strange
that i've won
and yet
lost.
well,
within the struggles of defeat
i conquered the fun and excitement
that comes throughout deciding,
just like a package deal—
nobody knows what's inside
and yet, they search for the right buy.
anticipating the outcome
you imagine the pleasure it'll bring—
and then once it's opened . . . presto
a complete waste.
you can't return it, so you chalk it up to experience.
now that you're aware
of the happiness gained before the outcome
you strive for that "surprise-package"
in everyday living—
humanity!"

"your game—
my name"

i have walked the ground
not you
i have made the rounds
not you
i have chose to lead my life this way
not you.

it's easier said than done
because
you have set me up
you have lessened my name
you have classified me as "abnormal."

but yet
it's my life

don't you remember—
freedom of choice—

no, i suppose you wouldn't
after all—
it's your world—
not mine!

Unspoken Emotions

YOUR WALK, TALK,
SMILE,
AND BODY—
EACH HAVE BEEN IMPLANTED
IN MY MIND . . . AND
MY EYES
HAVE BEEN TRAINED
TO PICK UP
ON EVERYTHING ABOUT YOU.
BEAUTY
IS NOT ONLY SKIN DEEP
EVEN THOUGH
I REALLY ENJOY
THE SURFACE FEATURES.
THERE'S A GLOWING LIGHT
THAT SHINES
AND FLOWS
AS YOU MOVE ABOUT.
THERE'S AN ELECTRICAL CHARGE
THAT YOU THROW OFF
EVERY TIME WE MEET.
THERE'S A LOVING BOND
SO STONG
THAT IT'S BECOME IMPOSSIBLE
TO BE BROKEN.

With Due Respect

ANTICIPATION
OF YOUR REACTION
AND
POSSIBLE ACCEPTANCE
AFTER ALL
I HAVE EXPOSED.

THE CLOSENESS
OF ANOTHER PERSON
THROUGH MUTUAL CARING,
WAS MINE
YESTERDAY—
BUT
IS THERE THE LEAST BIT
OF HESITANCE
TODAY?
THE WAITING . . .
WONDERING . . .
AND
WORRYING,
IS SO DIFFICULT A PROCESS
THAT I MUST
WAIT IT OUT!

Tranquility

And due to the finality of it all
you grow wiser & stronger
with each passing hour . . .
as you struggle to reach the depth of the inner most part of your soul.
And once there,
the calmness will lie
awaiting your arrival.
And once obtained
peace will be found
enabling you to end the traces
of the aforementioned pain
that has burdened your heart!

My Happiness

And throughout laughter
one says it all!
The fears and tears . . .
joys and memories . . .
wishing and wanting . . .
but
the most exciting
most stimulating,
most powerful laughter of all
is the one
given through
the eyes—
the one
and only one
that enables
as well as reveals
love.

Let it be me!

this is the time
when i felt the need to reach out
further than ever before—
grab onto your arm
and make you believe
that i'm not afraid
to show my love.
is it wrong
to show you how i feel?
i love you . . .
are you going to condemn me for it?
as the unknown answers
never perfectly clear
but always on the surface
making more progress
from day to day

i want you to see me as me
not as an image—
see me as i really am—
i won't hurt the slightest thing about your stance
just let me in . . . my way . . .
because if I can't show you
how can i let myself open up to anyone else

what will it be?

Desolate

Look into my eyes, and then tell me what's missing? It's gone isn't it? I saw it once before, but little do I know that it no longer exists. Has it slipped away from the warmth that surrounded it, or have you secured it where nobody can touch it, not even me? It was here just yesterday, but now it's gone . . . never to return. Please unlock it, for I'm gentle and loving. Nothing will change while it stays with me, safe in my memory . . . I give you my word. All I want to do is look upon it and relive beautiful memories that once existed. Don't you remember? It was just yesterday, but now it's gone, like a swift current pulling creation deep into a lifeless cell. Can't you see, without it I'm nothing but a mere skeleton!

Victorious?

Before I knew who you were,
game was the word.
A foul play here—
A wrong move there—
Never winning
but always undecided.
Should I
or shouldn't I?
It's either a clean sweep
or nothing at all.
What's there to lose?
It's only a game!

Something never thought of before
was that you can play
the game too.
It can knock you right out of the winners circle
and leave you with unforgotten scars.
It can do wonders—
just like another mind
predicating the outcome.

Between Spare Moments

burn me
break me
hurt me
hate me
and after you're completely satisfied
i'll still be here
in case you left something out,
can't you see
or don't you want to?
isn't it clear
for you make any connections?
i love—
i love you—
and if it means
Being used,
then here i am
at your disposal

all i want is happiness
and when you're around
i'm full of joy

so i'll take whatever you have to offer
and when you're not around
i'll wait
for you to call.

Leaves Turning Brazen

Did you ever look at a tree
and watch its branches extend out?
comparing it to a human being's life.
> "The bark is your protection
> The leaves are your loves
> The branches are your hands reaching out"
pleading for acceptance.
Did you ever look at a tree
and see yourself?
going in opposite directions—
trying to seek individuality.

Fragile Wings
up High

i love you
but i can't tell you
of my feelings
because if i do
i might appear
to be forcing the issue.

i can't explain the way i feel—
except that it's real

i just love you
to a degree
that i'm afraid.

Shattering Glass

To be touched
in such a special way
that the feelings inside
are constantly reproduced
without knowledge.
It's not caused by love
merely a touch
nothing more . . .
something that you could feel
like a gentile fingers talking.
what are they saying?
help me
use me
hurt me
i don't love
but need
something that everyone possesses
yet
i found it in you.

In the Beginning

I put out my hand
and you accepted without questions—
with that came my life.
A mass explosion of emotions—
I gave you every part of me:
My love
My hate
My dreams
but most of all
I gave you my most precious moments.
That is all I have—
and now its yours—
and even though,
you stand before me and say,
"What have you ever given me in return?"

White Socks And Other People

I love it, simply love it,—". . . and other people." Are the white socks superior? Hell yes! So, I have been told throughout my childhood. What more is there to elaborate on? Life in general is a very good beginning.

I speak so freely, and am the first to admit that I am prejudice. Believe me when I say that I'm not boasting, nor am I proud of the fact. Blaming the next guy for my ignorance seems like a good excuse that will be easily accepted by society, yet, there seems to be a flaw. Are we hypocrites?

Let's not get down on our fellow man. We are taught what our parents were taught. We somehow flow with the trend—partly out of inexperience in the socio-economical field, and partly not to defy our superiors.

Life goes on, and so do "white socks and other people." Unfortunately, we aren't going to make drastic changes to better understand our society—and thank goodness for that, because if perfection fell upon us, what would we write about?

Because Of You

CONSIDER IT DONE . . .
FOR TOGETHER
OUR MINDS
HAVE MERGED
IN FULL AGREEMENT
WITH OVERPOWERING
STRENGTH
TO GO THE ROUTE
OF EMOTIONAL DEPTH . . .
EXCLUDING TOUCH,
NERVOUSLY AWAITING
TO BE EXPLORED,
DUE TO A CONFLICT
OF
MORAL BELIEFS!

No Matter How Sad

It is only safe
to let memories of you
come to me in sunlight . . .
I have to be able to see
what's coming . . .
darkness disguises reality
it is all too easy
when I lay alone
to call up your touch
and let the sensation wash over my body . . .
daylight defers to distraction
a safety net to catch
the overflow of emotion . . .
the sun has become a friend
as it heals my body
with warmth
as if preparing me
for the dark
which will leave me empty and cold . . .

Caution: Dreams Crossing

So easy would it be for me
to walk the woods alone . . .
and sing to the sky, lost in thought,
while thinking of nothing at all.

And there's many days I like to sit
in the meadow all alone,
sipping on cheap wine
while dreaming of someone to love.

Other times I simply cuddle
near the fireplace all day long,
but quietly beneath the quilts
crying for someone to be near.

With jealous passion I've watched the clouds
drifting below the dusk
as if to kiss the sun goodnight.
Do you ever wonder where they spend the night?

Yes, more than once have I known this dream
but the ending never is clear.
Solitude seems all I want
Yet all I want seems empty without someone to be near.

Oh, let's walk the woods together
for we could still be quite alone.
Probably I'd sing to the sky while you pick the flowers
to decorate the mantel . . .

"a child"

The sensation hit
with an upward swing
and spun around
in a circular fashion
until solid ground was destined
by an overpowering impact.

Letting Go

i am walking out
not you
i am saying good-bye
not you
i am turning away,
leaving with a smile of hope
and a trace of guilt inside
because my time is over.

i am staring
not you
i am looking for strength
not you
i am full of last minute memories.

you are staying behind
moving in a similar direction
that the following year will bring

yet,

i am still me
and
you are the same person you've always been

i am on my way out
not you
i taking with me a joy that will live on a lifetime
not you,

and

if by chance
our lives should look down the same path
while passing through

i will extend my hand

and—
if you want

we can smile together once again.

What We Do For Love

Wave good-bye to the winds
as a storm hits the north eastern coast.
a smile
a terrible fight
or an innocent gesture.
it took four years to accomplish it
and it leaves in one day—
funny isn't it.
i suppose some people would say
"it isn't worth all the bothersome details"
but if you handed me four more years
the routine wouldn't be too much different.
somehow—
life needs what was given to me
a set back—
silence—
and most of all
people who care.
i lived it
and i'll miss it
but
it won't be forgotten.
sure it'll be revised
in years to come—
but it's almost impossible to recreate new contents
for words alone
seem to find a permanent place
in one's mind.

when i think about it
i want to laugh—
you know?
i never had to walk out first
because the other person always beat me to it—
but now it's my turn
and i should be happy …
maybe i really am
and don't know it yet.
sure, that's it
"only I don't know it".

Your perception
overwhelms my instincts
during troubled times

To overlook your struggling determination
Putting emphasis
on conquering
the central phase
of destruction
as you see fit

Posing the question
of possible defeat
never enters into the situation
since
the strength within your own mind
has the capacity
of towering over
the abuser—
But . . .
always be aware
of potential downfalls
which hinder & devastate
a competitive goal

Totality

I can't speak for you
but as I see it
life is too short
to let happiness pass it by.
a kind word
or a sincere smile
serves the purpose,
tomorrow's another day
with different wants and desires
but for today
i'm content!

Make Believe

you've become an enormous mental block—
with each train of thought
existing throughout my mind.
i speak silent words
to the images i've created
of you.

sometimes
you answer me
when i think deep enough

"nothing like good old wish fulfillment"!

regardless . . .
you're here
with me
in a world of
dreams and fairytales.

"all at once"

Not knowing what to do when times go bad
one turns to man in distress—
loving becomes stronger
and hate appears somewhat superficial
for help is a means of calmness.
we cannot survive by ourselves alone
because mankind is all around to assist us in our journey.
people are love
love is you
and
you are once again lost in hopelessness.
to find relief
you must face the pain
and before you can face what has happened
you will have to strive to understand why you are doing so.
within yourself a solution can be found
but not unless the hurt is dealt with.
somehow it's like rain
once the storm strikes,
its length is undetermined, or
until the rainbow shines throughout,
offsetting the clouds
unbiased to the universe!

The Haunting Never Ends

To my knowledge
the human race is somewhat broken
in a world of constant change—
dreadful bombings
mass murders
and
governmental scandals
in every form imaginable.
no stopping—
pure greed—
we live in hopes of a new beginning
but our chances are limited
of seeing any less bitterness
because we have no authority
over powers above and beyond reach.

The Competition

It is exhilarating
when winning reaches your way
however, when it gets into one's head
nervousness becomes
polluted with greed
and you lose all rationalization
of actuality.
it is like a streak of bad luck.
you begin to think
that life forgot to include you—
however, if you stick it out
through the good times as well as the bad,
there will be a certain
feeling of pride
from inside
and respect from bystanders
throughout.

falling to where?

Climbing
without the use of my hands
i grasped onto the winds
that surrounded my body, and trembled:
as the earth shook the atmosphere within—
my steel beams were struck . . . before i had a chance to repent.
not to you
but to myself
for becoming taller than my fellow man
who is my equal.

. . . a smile, some harsh words, and total contentment—

knowing that you cried
remembering the last words spoken
"not when you need"
listening to that confident voice over the phone
and then a dial tone—
it all seems so far away
like a dream of the past
or a figment of one's imagination
but needless to say, it's reality.
extend your hand
to reassure me
that the fright inside
is unimportant
and the moments ahead will be good ones.
a quote which you recited
stands distinctly in my mind
one that says:
"i can't help you"
but that's not all
there something else—
. . . a smile, some harsh words, and total contentment—
they convey a puzzle,
you.
Most memories are truly beautiful
and also rewarding
then again
i touch on those which cause misery—
one being of my past attitude towards you

it still hurts me
but i couldn't talk to you
because there was a desperate need—
i respect your wishes
and therefore refrained from what i wanted.

sometimes i laugh
at those emotions
that eat the hell out of us.
it is really remarkable
how they prevent letdowns
or bring tears to one's eyes.
"so you see
i'm feeling those emotions right now
and it's hard to detect what they're saying
because i'm uncertain of my own thoughts."

Mirrored Reflections

Revisions
of a day gone by—
sight
without the use of my eyes
but with a sense
obtained through adversity
in order to live once again.
that extra touch
to see future happenings
in a matter of seconds.
searching
in order to survive
years from now.
reaching out
to those few people
who will be left
when all others have been destroyed.
all consistency and perception wasted
so that one final person
can predict a moment of truth
without fear.

if you were my mommy

Tell me—
how do you like me
you've known me for almost a minute
and still—
you hardly said a word.
i can tell our future
we'll play in the park
and throw pebbles in the ocean
maybe—
we can get daddy to take us for a ride
just because he loves us/
sometimes—
i might even ask you for a penny
to buy a gum ball
or
if i'm lucky
you'll give me a shiney new dime
for an ice cream cone.
oh i'm so excited about us sharing
my entire childhood
it's just beginning
and i can see beautiful times ahead—
for both of us
daddy too.

mommy
when i get big
i always want to see you smile
like you do when your all happy.
know what i mean—
like after you get when daddy
says "i love you"

i don't know what else to say
except that someday
when i become noticed
i will point you out
and state that
"i love you".

Follow through the towering skies, up upon an opening to man. it's not hard to detect, but one must have experience in traveling vicious circles if he wishes to be successful in his journey. One can't call it "follow the leader" due to unwanted emotional pressures. travel at your own rate of speed, be conscious of detours purposely planted to catch your attention. they're unimportant-ignore them. if you wish to pause along the way that's your choice but keep safe within your own mind and existence. you're never completely lost if you hold onto yourself. once that is gone, destruction arrives next. many years may pass before you cover the slightest amount of territory but as soon as possible you shift into high gear. There's no telling when you'll stop.

This trip is exciting and educational, and therefore; worth one's time. It may be labeled essential to those who find life interesting enough to look into its surrounding & atmosphere. If you have your own personal doubts, attempt a little at a time. Don't step into it all at once unless you are prepared for the unknown outcome. Strangely enough, if you're without a solution, the next person might trap you within his miraculous powers capable of haunting the hell out of your soul. This way of survival is tricky, risky, and somewhat dangerous therefore increase your stability in search of motivation.

Now that the explanation for making yourself be put out on a limb, it has been clearly justified, much luck will also be needed. If one lacks the will of wit, he has a great deal of work cut out for himself. Just take it easy and don't rush into anything. There aren't any time limits to your behavior in exploring the universe!

A Laugh, A Smile or Two, Some Tears, And a Circle

i wish i could sing a hundred words
or fly like a wild bird
and cry out to the skies
that the things i've said
would be heard—
just like walking in the rain
soaked from head to toe—
water dripping down the sides of my cheeks
inspiring all of which i know—
a summer breeze
wisping about my hair
forming somewhat of a blinder
except for the spot from which i can see
all happiness and love—
sometimes looking at a black dot
watching it revolve
becoming larger with each glance
but never fading!
i watch each and every one of these
and at times i reach out my hand
with the knowledge that
it will sometimes be rejected—
but i've got to let it out once more
because i need something that can be touched!

You looked at me
this morning
and my entire body trembled.
i felt limp
a tightness formed in my throat
and with that
i became speechless
all i was able to do was
stare at your presence
i couldn't even say
"hello"
somehow—
a grin escaped
and as usual
you returned it
i'm sorry
really sorry
that i didn't offer you
anything more
than my shaky stance.

if we could see far enough in advance
would the outcome be in our favor?
if death was patterned like a lottery
would we back out when our turn came?
if we were capable of picking our wants
what could we possibly strive for?
would anyone care?
would there be pain or sorrow—
permanently!

it sounds so easy
and yet
our minds could never consume the decisions.
if we decided to try
we'd laugh at our own ignorance.

wouldn't it be much more effective
to accept life with each passing day—
instead of wasting our intelligence
by grasping onto the future
before it comes—

tomorrow
is a mystery.
it gives way to those few who can
psych out all other sources.
it spreads rumors
that hold no truth—
it fights like hell
in order to preserve one more life—
it makes you cry
to see what impulses do.
you awake
to an entirely different surrounding
and become just a trifle bit smarter—
because you see not what you want
but what's realistic
in the standings of today's society.

Death—
Destruction—
Pain—
Life without a beginning
No ties or strings attached
Nothing.

Sin where no crime was committed
Prayers when nobody will hear
Tears because of a day gone by.

Hell
Over and over again
With a laughing audience
To guide you along.

It's bitter
But that's what happens
When we give up hope.

"Evergreen"

If by chance
you hear them call out my name
don't be the first to run.
Let the hands of time
tick away
while your mind is still fresh—
for nothing will be lost
if you decide to live
before you recognize death.
It's not an offensive word
yet, it devastates many hearts
without meaning to do so.
Keep it hidden
in the darkness
until you can look at it objectively—
not as pain
but as a rebirth
of life
that was taken
in order to initiate another mind to provide accomplishments,
that were unable to be fulfilled.

A fine line running through
"who" you are
and
"what" you represent

The distinction,
sometimes appearing vague,
lacks insight . . .
allowing a definite parallel
to merge into one . . .
creating a barrier for separation
in determining
the allowances
for such a split
to occur
without reservation

Portraying, as well as preserving
Two distinct entities,
becomes overwhelming
once "Personal emotion"
over-rides
professionalism
causing an altercation of viewpoint.

"Deep In Thought"

DEEP-INTENSE
LOVE-HATE
WANT-NEED-DEVOTION

I WANT

LOVE YOU VERY MUCH
SEE YOU SMILE
HOLDING OUT MY HAND
WANTING TO TOUCH
SEEING PAIN STRIKE

LOVE IS DYING

I WANT TO BE WITH YOU
GIVE
I WON'T HURT
PLEASE BELIEVE ME—FOR ONCE
PURSUE THE ISSUE

EVIL

YEARNING INSIDE
BE ME
DON'T PULL BACK
TAKE MY HAND
HUG
LET ME SEE A TEAR
OF JOY—
OR REGRET

GOOD-BYE.

wave good-bye to the winds
as a storms comes ahead.
a smile
a terrible fight
or an innocent gesture.
it took four years to accomplish it
and it leaves in one day—
funny isn't it.
i suppose people would say
"it isn't worth all the bothersome details"
but if you handed me four more years
the routine wouldn't be too much different.
somehow—
life needs what was given to me
a set back—
silence—
and most of all
people who care.
i lived it
and i'll miss it
but
it won't be forgotten.
sure it'll be revised
in years to come—
but it's almost impossible to recreate a new contents
for words alone
seem to find permanent place
in one's mind.

when i think about it
i want to laugh—
you know?
i never had to walk out first
because the other person always beat me to it—
but now it's my turn
and i should be happy . . .
maybe i really am
and don't know it yet.
sure, that's it
only . . .
i don't know it.

QUIET DAYS AND QUIET NIGHTS
AND STILL I CRY.
ALONE AT LAST
TO FILL THE VAST CONFUSION
AND I GO HALF
OUT OF MY MIND.

TO HEAR THE SOUNDS
OF MY OWN HEART BEAT
AND THE PITTER-PATTER
OF MY FEET
FROM UNDERNEATH MY CHAIR.

AND SILENCE

<u>GOLDEN</u> SILENCE
GRASPS HOLD OF MY LIFE
ONCE AGAIN
AS I TRY TO CATCH MY BREATH
BEFORE IT SUFFOCATES
MY INNER BEING . . .
THAT I AM!!!

The Stairway

TRANQUILITY
CALMNESS
INNER-PEACE
THE THIRST AND HUNGER FOR SUCH BEAUTY
IS REVEALED IN TOTALITY
DOWN THE STAIRWAY.
(THROUGHOUT THE CAPACITY OF ONE'S MIND)

A TWENTY-FOUR SECOND "HIGH" SHARED BY NONE OTHER
THAN HE WHO PARTAKES.
IT'S BREATH-TAKING, YET DARING
EMOTIONAL, YET COLD

BUT IN THE FINAL STAGES OF THAT BLANK STARE,
REVEALED THROUGH THE EYES,
A REWARDING CHILL RUSHES THROUGHOUT
ONE'S ENTIRE BODY, NEVER TO BE FORGOTTEN.

A SIGNIFICANT PIECE OF LIFE HAS BEEN CAPTURED.

Why do people have to love
more than one person—
not all require it
but enough—

when your depressed
i'm sad
when you cry
I have the urge to.

You stand there
looking so helpless—
i want to reach out and help
but something holds me back.
for the time being
lets call it fright.

i would like to do so many things—
most of all
put a smile on your face
but not unless it's sincere!
you see—
the most i can do is to tell you "i care"
and hope that you believe me.

"Ain't Life Grand!!!"

For this I will build upon
as it's of extreme importance
to me . . .

Over the past few days
your smile has radiated
the room of your presence,
And I
have felt the depth of that smile
in its entirety!!!
I've also allowed myself to be touched
by emotion
where normally
I'd have shunned the opportunity.
Why?
I've asked myself the same question,
There is a very strong force
that comes from within
your very soul,
that's only permitted to surface
on your own personal request.
It is similar to engaging in a
"mind game . . ."
so stimulating
that for the period of time
it takes to participate
you allow your thought pattern
total freedom.

Isn't it amazing
what an individual can think
as long as he never surfaces
those thoughts
into words!!!

"yes—they're ours"

What's happening to the children?
they're slowly turning away
in search for an open heart
to grasp onto
with the notion of never letting go.
who is to blame?
are we neglecting their essential needs
by ignorance—
or are they afraid of devastation
as individuals.
how can they experience liberation
in a changing, world.
revolving in opposite directions.
at a rate of speed
unknown to man's knowledge.
will there ever come a time
when our assistance
can draw them closer
to a point in life
that we may share together once more.

my past
has become
a faint shadow
and all i can see
is that beautiful smile
you've somehow created
so effectively.

One Very Sincere Thought

I want to see you,
. . . spend time with you,
. . . love you,
without stipulations.
The urgency,
to express
everything I am experiencing inside
has set a precedent
for the immediate.
I long to touch,
. . . feel,
. . . intertwine,
our bodies mutually . . .
without question.
Your mere presence
manifests
an engulfment
that overpowers my natural instincts
to preserve and protect
the person that I am.
Slowly,
ever so slowly,
I am beginning to feel as though
the two of us
are merging
into one!!!

" . . . *Blank Stares* "

Beyond the wall, I have no name, merely visions of yesterdays. Is it mystification that holds my attention or an accumulation of curiosity obtained throughout the use of my senses?

Beyond the wall, I have no name, simply memories and second guesses. However, to my surprise, life's not filled with endless "highs", rather the potential for deceit and false pretenses.

Beyond the wall is not an elective, nor desire longing to be fulfilled; instead, an experience based on honesty that allows a permanent impression . . . coinciding with future accomplishments, not yet obtained.

> What is the purpose, if a prerequisite entails a traumatic experience enabling one's inner strength to become debilitating?

I have witnessed the safety as well as gratification, in "The Wall", for as I view the capabilities within its confines, the observer has the option to walk away if the outlook becomes too explicit. On the other hand, "Beyond" is transitional, evolving without an alternate outline to formulate a counter offer if challenged.

As a helpless entity,
we are conditioned to choose situations that are capable of creating happiness, contentment and minimal physical and/or mental exertion, to overcome barriers. It has been instilled in our minds that invalidation is a requirement for those few who aren't afraid to touch life, feeling its impact ignite the essence for that which constitutes reality.

In retrospect, a great injustice would be done to those individuals who sought escape from a predetermined mode of conditioning, by classification inferior to the remainder of humanity. Mass confusion cannot be adequately deciphered without a strategic mind to unravel the rewards, which would otherwise remain dormant.

Beyond the wall, one has no name . . . only memories and second guesses. Too bad that didn't read "second chances"!

Do Not Let Them Be Like Mine, I Beg Of Thee

Trust and be trusted . . .
hate and be loved . . .
hurt and be used . . .
live without death!

what more can be asked
if you're not willing to explore
in order to perfect life?
give whenever possible
and receive without question—
however not on a regular basis.
be objective
and evaluate your thoughts.
do not jump to conclusions
before they transpire
and always remember—
to protect what's yours
so that tomorrow won't be spent
in vein!

only one minute

"to look back—
gazing upon the laughter of a single thought
seeing pain strike
with a professional touch
seeking opportunities which bring
a lifeless cell overpowering wit
revealing a need for assistance
without motivation."
what's all the pounding . . .
existing between heart beats?
impatience due to reality . . .
or fright from the untold truth?
"let go
for only one minute
without any means of communication
be yourself and see."
is it an excuse
or an escape
a desperate hate
or an unwanted love.
look—gaze—stare
all in only one minute.

Translucent Love

Need is a small word
that holds indefinite limitations.
want moves along right next to it
when our eyes become attached.
hope is a virtue
we try to capitalize on.
understanding is too long a word to say
during times of impatience.
dreams are admirable
when they lead us to our goals.
happiness is a giving process
shared by everyone
love will continually be the key word
every one of us strive to obtain!

Against The Multi-Colored Skies

reflect upon the good times
when happiness
cast a rainbow
in the center of two people in love.
brightness
from the rays of the sun
shone directly on their faces
adding a special glow to their smiles
microphones
planted on their bodies
picking up soft tones
of future plans together—
thunder—
lightening—
rain—
a total black out
tomorrow is another day
to discover love.

you amaze me
even though i tell myself
"expect the unexpected."
a smile
excitement in your voice
and some harsh words
become a pattern from day to day
but still
you leave room for something else—
i suppose it comes natural
yet
it can't be labeled—
one might refer to it
as a guessing game . . .
"what's next?"
will it be a
burst of enthusiasm?
a sudden tear?
or total contentment-?
we're all waiting to find out
and at times
I think
you are too!

****

There are times like now, when I'd like to take off with no intentions of returning. I can't see myself standing by one's side who constantly finds trivial situations more important than everything else in the world. It is a waste of time and great emotional strain not worth experiencing.

I try viewing the problem at hand with an open mind, but there are times when nothing can be done to see what another sees with objectivity. Such as the present. You cannot depend on outside help at the very moment you may need a favor. I fully understand what priorities you hold on the matter, but others also have priorities that do not coincide with yours. It isn't anybody's fault for this and yet you are ready to kill. This is when I want to wipe my hands clean.

It almost makes me laugh, because I've been drawn into a fight pertaining to something I have no power to correct. Why?

I now realize something very interesting. In order to maintain peace of mind as well as peace between two of us, I am supposed to keep myself on reserve for your desired wants . . .

Sorry to inform you of this but I don't care for the arrangement you've managed to create. If you can't do better next time around find yourself another fool. I quit!

With All My Love

There was a lonely corner in my world until you smiled at me from a distance. With that extension of your open arms, I took with me something that will never be easily put completely out of my mind.

Somehow I can still feel the overwhelming sensation of those precious moments. Maybe you viewed it differently than I had wanted you to, because those feelings can become disillusioning when one falls into despair . . . (without realization?)

The next time our paths cross I will be careful in making any gestures that could be misleading to either one of us.

When making the same mistake twice, stop the end of the first before beginning the second.

Emotional Overload

Please help me in my struggle
to accept the difficulties
I am encountering,
even though
my actions may be
without justification.
By listening to my words,
you will detect my fears
and,
while they, too,
may be without cause,
they're very real to me.
Hold me, without questions
and let me feel your strength
for only then, will I be at peace.

"Searching for the Unknown"

Trying to reach out, looking to find something not visible, but rewarding. It's nothing to be found, since it lies objectless. Meditation may reveal it if one exposes his inner and outer soul—and connects them. Man can't find clues or be "led on" to this mysterious being, since he isn't aware of his actual powers. You are now involved in playing a game. Searching for the unknown.

I suppose time takes its strides with slow, revolving seconds—millions of them. You sweat it out, without physical movement in the least. Any minute, you're ready to burst, mentally. There's little left inside of that dreary body, but if you should happen to give in, it's all over. In all fairness, what can possibly be done? If man knew the answer, he would have revealed it way before our time. But then again, if man could detect the "mysterious something" he wouldn't need a way out!

"all at once"

Not knowing what to do when times go bad
one turns to man in distress—
loving becomes stronger
and hate seems to somewhat disappear
for help is a means of desperation.
we cannot survive on ourselves alone
because humanness is all around
people are love
love is you
and
you are once again lost in desperation.
to find a cure
you must face the pain
and before you can face what has happened
you strive to know why.
within yourself a solution can be found
but not unless the hurt comes through.
somehow it's like rain
once the storm hits
it's uncontrollable
until
the clouds become neutral
impartial to all creation.

my mind is heavy, yet free

You are becoming more
meaningful in my life
with each passing day—
i realize it often,
yet deny my feelings
as usual!
i have learned
in past experiences
that "I" don't always
reveal the real person
"i" stand for
unless "i" am willing
to accept the consequence.
"i" approve of my emotional contents
yet
not always willing
to expose it to the other person.
so
without saying a word
know
by my actions
just how very special
you are to me!

Why do we always fight
with those few
who are so close to us

why are there always ends
but very seldom
do new beginnings occur
soon enough
for good happenings to enter

why are you staring in the mist of all this?

are you seeing beyond me?

If we could see far enough in advance
would the outcome be in our favor?
if death was patterned like a lottery
would we back out when our turn came?
if we were capable of picking out our wants
what could we possibly strive for?
would anyone care?
would there be pain or sorrow—
or would the lid be shut
permanently!

it sounds so easy
and yet—
our minds could never consume the decisions.
if we decided to try
we'd laugh at our own ignorance.

wouldn't it be much more effective
to accept life with each passing day—
instead of wasting our intelligence
by grasping onto the future
before it comes?

It might become a joke
after you have snapped out of an emotional state
but you know damn well
there will be another
time when you turn to it for comfort . . . .

For,
once in awhile occurrences
will become everyday happenings!

The Gift of Sharing

Yes,
Gentleness
And warmth . . .
You took my breath away right from the start.
With your openness . . .
Your belief in yourself . . .
And your apparent trust in me.
I love you so dearly
For what you have given to me.
Freely
Without doubt or hesitation.
My love
You will never be forgotten,
For deep within my heart
I will always know that you're near
And will not let me falter
As I walk down
The path . . . .
Never again to be
Alone.

My Unknown Boundaries

I'm terribly afraid of losing your friendship due to my level of caring. Believe me when i say that i'm fantastic at maintaining all the outer control necessary, for your eyes to capture. I've done remarkable in past experiences, but with you, I want to be honest. It wouldn't be worth it to even attempt to lie where you're concerned.

I unnecessarily worry, but at times, with moderate justification. My former therapist, has tried desperately to get me to set a limit/boundary where you're concerned. as she quoted to me, i will do the same for you: "we can love our friends dearly, and share in intimate relationships, (not to be mistaken as sexually) that are sacred and rewarding." my problem is that i never set boundaries <u>ever</u> before in my life! this might sound crazy, but i truly don't know how. i'm serious. i never want to hurt you, yet i'm overly cautious not to offend you in any way—can one of the two care too greatly, and still maintain a balance in the relationship?

Let Our Children Survive

In the calm
of the eastern winds
violence breaks out
and blood marks the point of all evil.
nothing to be accomplished
but in-depth damage
to that of one's mind and soul.
peace—
an unfamiliar word
to man on earth.
pain and sorrow—
fantastic!
because it fits right into the mold
of everyday living.

Joyful Memories

to be able to touch the very finest in life
to let it slip through your fingers
without hesitation
capturing beauty within . . .
not blinking an eye lash
or shedding a tear
because nothing is lost
if the finest has been experienced.
you don't have to keep it
or even enjoy it to its fullest—
simply explore the unfamiliar surroundings
and soon
they will be made history
in a life that you created.
just let it be known
that you didn't let life pass you by
before you made an indentation
with the palm of your hand
and a wound in your heart . . .
that felt love.

dreams

A smile
a curiosity
a possible want
to experiment
doubt
and once again
curiosity—
too easy a dream
too willing a person
dreams
should have remained
in the minds
of children.

As I sit back and think of the times of corruption, my mind wanders from person to person. All the innocence drains from the person I am, and guilt fills my veins. I suppose nothing has occurred that serious to destruct with such a powerful impact, but looking at pain with a light touch doesn't seem realistic. Pressure pours on as I review, and memories become brighter than the most beautiful sunrise. It all depends on one's images of life—if you love, you love harder— and when you hate, it's with an overpowering passion. Strange! Life is somewhat strange when you find so many paths that are filled with love—real love. That is what you call life's little pains. You can try leveling it out, but there are no guarantees. It's your world—make it the best you can.

Take it or Leave It

And the wheels keep on spinning
with the mockery and lies
cheating and disbelief
but there's always room
for the free—
existing in a world of give and take.
The simple one
the real one—
Don't get me wrong
I'm not saying the perfectionist
but that of a true to life person.
Not a phony!
A big "hi"—"go to hell"—"oh, shit"
are typical expressions
and surprisingly enough
they're natural.
It's amazing how this world finds the time
for true people—
but then again
nothing is shocking
when it comes to man.

This can't be true, but explainable in various types of emotional outbursts. It's obvious that tempers beam out, yet project themselves in a somewhat mannerly way. Concentration and logic prove positive in this case, for one's mind must control impulsive flashbacks as quickly as they occur. Your face usually reveals the true feelings inside, but protects the position you maintain throughout the entire day.

Facial structures begin to form into great masterpieces, unable to be legally framed. It's not a figment of your imagination, simply a beautifully painted picture. I see it, for within my mind, I've created it as I see fit. You might see a smile—or a sudden tear. I detect aggravating frustration. What can be done to stop it? Maybe a little consideration or preparation. I don't know the answer as completely as I'd like to, for I speak as the minority. That's not enough to clearly justify my statement, but it's a damn good start!